HIDDEN SEQUEL

For Greg
with great admiration
and great joy
in your music
in your friendship
Run/Play in your [?]

8.9.13

Winner of the Barrow Street Press Poetry Prize
selected by Donald Revell

HIDDEN SEQUEL

Stan Sanvel Rubin

Barrow Street Press
New York City

Designed by Robert Drummond

Cover photo:Mikael Levin

Published by Barrow Street Press
Distributed by:
      Barrow Street
      P.O. Box 1831
      Murray Hill Station
      New York, NY 10156

First Edition

Library of Congress control number: 2006901476

ISBN 0-9728302-5-1

for J., of course

Contents

I. The Door

II. Hunters

III. Laws of Silence

No, my heart is not sleeping,
It is awake. Awake.
                    —Machado

I. THE DOOR

They are rejoicing over the atom bomb.
Only now, they claim, is eternal peace dawning....
How miserable, how blind, how incapable
of learning from experience are these
human animals. Out of the fear of death,
they proclaim everlasting peace.

                                —Wilhelm Reich, journal entry, 7 August 1945

A

The capital of desire, the shortcut,
the road to a name that is stuttered
in a shower of sparks that is cast out
forward and backward like a demon
dispossessed from the elements
seeking a home among humans,
it will find you in the quick uncivilized
breaths between breathing, the automatic
music of the skeleton twisting, the cries
of a mother who has no time cry out
the names of her children forged in an instant
into one name, a long wail, a melody, a huge
unheard eloquence: the sacred redacted to shadow
on a bridge between nowhere and here
Who, if I cried out, would hear me? Rilke asks

Door

"War Dims Hope For Peace"
-from 2004's Best (Actual) Headlines

It's inevitable, isn't it, that the bulb
in the bathroom is still on
when you go to bed exhausted,
that, slipping between cool sheets,
you can see the phosphorescent lines
of a doorway lit from within,
the blinding outline of light
etching itself into your retina
like an image from Hiroshima

so that you cannot sleep, try as you
might, you cannot close
your eyelids tight enough
to pretend it isn't there,
that thin sketch of illuminated shadow
like rice paper burning,
that patch of nothing suddenly beckoning
through nothing, that hole
in the night, that other doorway.

Variations in the Key of Night

I am open to the night
because the door is open.

You left the door open
and did not turn on the light.

When you entered, shadows entered,
irresolute as light.

Now nothing is certain,
because the dark walked in

with you, trailing you,
leading you with its embrace.

You did not chase
the night with a shut door,

a turned-on light
when you came in.

When you came in
the night arrived

deliberate as a Bedouin
through a glare of sand

to a distant mountain
he can barely trace,

as carefully as that you came
to my waiting hand.

Night Light

To remain asleep in this world
you must close your mind to riddles,

you must close your eyes
to the dance of corpses that are everywhere,

you must close your ears
to their insistent cries

blatant as insults yelled
across a parking lot after a game.

You must begin to assume the pose
of a connoisseur of shadows,

you must contemplate your own happiness
like the jewel of your life,

think of it now, think of the ways
you can be happy,

the varieties of happiness
so many precious orchids,

how you will one day grow to fill
the position of an expert

on your own happiness,
you will forget what woke you

this time, what kept you sleepless.
Can you feel it now, the rest, the gratification,

the deep breath of peace?

Man on Deck

This ship is important to him
because somewhere in its lower depths
he hears the sound of his own breathing,
an engine clanking, clanking,
driving the ship on, all the gears grinding,
expenditure of force making
a hash of noise so that he cannot
hear himself think for more than a second
unless he looks beyond the shape of starlit waves
to the wide sea without edges

where, standing and staring there
like a seabird born to the sea
with the whole world its circumference,
oblivious to the challenge of fire
because in its dancing it is fire,
he forgets the sounds under his feet,
the skeletal pipes and funnels and valves,
the maze of mechanical accomplishment
that runs invisibly everywhere and remembers
the feeling of first voyage, the shore he has left.

Three Scars

This is a strip of memory,
a voice pulled like a cart through a gate of skin
until skin surrenders, for an instant,
its tight periphery.

This is the shadow of breath,
an expected blow that didn't come,
a voice stopped in mid-sentence by
another voice.

This is the imprint
of a deeper wound,
a word that still races in the blood,
the epic stallion.

Driving Home During the Eclipse

Nature's dark side is heeded now–
            —Herman Melville, "Misgivings"

Round as a fist, ruined circle, clown
with no face, withered
cloud brittle as anger,
stripped of itself the moon
tries to blend into earthshadow

which won't hold it
as we round bend after bend
beneath the stiff white-tipped mountains
where Skagit Valley opens
in a pantomime

of what won't hold us—
flat fields, two hands held
side by side to balance
what we keep trying to read life into,
love and its hidden sequel.

The Lie

i.

I didn't mean what you heard
—the hurtful lines, the story
I thought was true. *If you said it,*
you meant it, you say.

ii.

As much as—and this is what
we don't tell anyone—we'd like
to lose ourselves in the stream of words
and ride it to wherever it goes,
we know it can't go on forever,

this ingenuity of syllables,
this hypnotic authority of song.
Listen, even the rude monk
awake with his wine
hears the early birds calling,

senses the disaster of morning.

iii.

It was one of those odd moments—
whatever I wanted was wrong,
whatever I was accused of
I had done.

iv.

In the ideal state, poems
won't exist (you know
Plato's argument),
only the real, perfectly
exposed to light.

History, probably, will end.
Stalin, after news of
the death of Gorky,
his old pal and fellow
Bolshevik, slept well.

What he'd planned had worked.
What he'd ordered was done.
He was accused of nothing,
not even innocence.
This, in its own way, is art.

The Stain

i.

All night, I lay with the dead
They had calm, peaceful faces

Their pasts sifted like dust through wiry bones
Their grasping fingers settled for nothing

They stared at me as if they stared at no one
In the morning they were gone

And I was here

ii.

All night the dead lay around me
It was like a battlefield, only costlier

The dead were spliced together, a movie of the dead
They didn't recognize

the stars that sighed into their sockets
or the slow ox of morning moving toward us

iii.

What is petrified is what was once flowing
What is flowing will stall like an eclipse

This is what made me falter in the morning,
reaching for coffee

This might have been called a vision, once

The Lost

The dead and the lost have the same dream.
Lying in a hard bed, you find them
twined in shadows, twinned in desire,
doubled like music that repeats itself,
endlessly, always needing more.

The mad and the lonely are ancient lovers.
Shadows watch them and shadows walk
with them wherever they go walking.
It's a long way to go and they will never make it.
It's too far to go and they know it.

Object/Lessons

i.

If you think you love justice,
poetry may be only
a way of despairing.

ii.

The man who shoots
at another man has forgotten
what the student who sits all day
is trying to remember.

iii.

The one who dies
dies, of course, for all of us.
That's the irony,
because we're not all one,
we don't even want to be.

iv.

Some of us want death
the way flies want rotten meat.

v.

Others, however hard
it is to admit in a poem,
need death, its implements,
because, yes, they carry it.

Photo of a Field at the Start of a Century

This is not a painting,
these numbskull boys
with frost smeared across their lips,
eyes burnt open, staring
at us as they lie twisted
in the pile they were left in,
not waiting to rise again
and walk unthinking toward
the disease or law or animal
that would beat them down to bone.

Here there is no other story
to imagine—we cannot count
their losses: the years of grain
they will not bend to harvest,
the fists of alcohol they will not drink
to rouse themselves to hoarse joy
when the fields are stripped,
the sweating, the fucking, the cries,
the intricate hatreds they already wore
when they were laid here, suddenly

tribeless, anonymous, without regret,
a field themselves covering a field.

To Return

We returned, all of us, in time for the last
fire on the Straits, the water burning,
the late sails burning, the islands
sinking in orange flames.

We returned, some of us rushing
inside, the pop and rattle
of cookery splitting the quiet
with the small mechanics of evening.

We returned, you standing alone
on the shore as if the silence, the waves
and the sunset were a single sentence
we might read forever, despite the night.

II. HUNTERS

Hunters

the gods are wind and death and thunder and the buttery slime of birth
—Albert Goldbarth, *Worlds*

When the gods are happy, they hunt you
with their happiness,
they pursue you
with the frenzy of sharks,
a gang of mutts
going after a sick cat
in an alley
When the gods are unhappy,
they attempt all ways to cancel you
They settle in your brain
and in your pants
Your nose leaks with them
Rape and torment
are their tiniest achievements

So duplicity
is the way we know ourselves,
marionettes run through
with strings,
barges pulled through fog
by distant tugboats
too far ahead to see
Every nerve responds to them,
placed as it is in perfect conjunction
to their whims, their utterances
of casual, meaningless breath
that can blow us off course, maybe forever,
on a map no one can read

Stoop

Once I was welcome in a house.
Then I was not.

It's hard to fathom
being unwelcome

after so many years,
so long a stay as honored guest.

The anticipated hospitality
of familiar rooms

replaced
by sliding shadows.

The warmth of words
by the clamor

of hidden windows shutting,
the chill of daylight silence.

How maddening, at night,
to count for nothing,

to go unnoticed
this time, and always.

Intolerable, really, to be
as lost as the winds.

After all you endured,
not even to be told.

The Trace

i.

Plotinus says the soul
carries a spark
that illumines everything.

He did not start to write
until fifty years old,
a teacher in Rome

whose *house was full
of young lads and maidens*
according to Porphyry,

who also tells us the philosopher
could never bear to reread
what he had written down:

*Even to read it through once
was too much for him.*

ii.

I carry a dented flashlight.
I pace the house,
looking for signs.

Domesticity scars these walls.
I could be walking
through our life again.

This is not
the patience of saints
but the mission

of a sleepless man
who must reread
what body has written.

iii.

*He seemed ashamed
to be in the body,* Porphyry
begins.

Seventeen centuries
later, Yeats asked
for a soul that will not

bruise the flesh.
I bend at the toaster
oven to inspect

a line of mouse leavings
scribbled across the shelf
toward a shadowy corner

where floor meets the wall.
He's there, brother
who steals my sleep.

iv.

I'll leave a trap tonight
baited with sour havarti
to lure the creeping messenger

with his own sharpened
hunter's senses
that betray.

Rope

Starved for flesh
it loops the neck
with its braided
kiss innocent
as grass woven
into basket, into net
in which pale salmon twist.

Gun

Those who have fired upon others
in anger or despair,
embracing the slick metal
of the barrel, sliding
the index finger
back with the curved trigger,
leaning into the kill,

understand the power
of cure, the way
desire becomes
annihilation, the way
action obliterates
the unbreakable strands of pain
love connects to everything.

Pipe

It's blunt as lead
aimed at your head.

It's what you meant,
not what you said.

LAWS OF FLIGHT: I

I desire the things which will destroy me in the end.
                    —*The Unabridged Journals of Sylvia Plath*

It takes the gravity of a moth
to forget what happened
last time you believed
it could work: the re-
discovered innocence
of Rilke's *Third Elegy*,

the Prometheus'
skirting of power,
the Luna's
pale green resurrections
from flame
until the final

wavering eccentric orbit
into the very center
where the salty buds open,
the heart itself
become magnificent,
a transitory brilliance of failure.

.

I'm proof that everything ends
that both whiskey and labor
have a time, an appointed rhythm
of waning. I have
no twin and need none.
You cannot see past me.

The moon shrivels to this,
as does dust, as do worlds.

—

Prod, clipper, stickman
who died, or at least
is seriously sick
enough to fall flat here
after flailing for connection

( )
I'm as strong as air
when it nuzzles the tip of a candle
then extinguishes

I'm the wings of nothing, containing
an infinite vacuum god

,

and on and on and on and on and on and on and

Laws of Flight: II

Breath held beyond limit
emptied between planets
You are now the only

wing, the illegible secret
connecting
dark to dark, light to light.

You are everywhere
Is this why they named you
pilferer, lean throat, crow?

Laws of Flight: III

Not to understand how you got here
because of the moon's torrent,
its dizzy impassible bridges and strings
elastic, suddenly, with room to burn
the sling between stars

tunnel and arc of breath, the tooth
of dog star angrily spitting fire
but dimming, dimming, so that you
under that weird eye might pass,
as you do now,

unstirrupped and serene.

Lunch

for Ana Menendez

Certain saffron dishes woke the city.
Peeling layers of frost from tomatoes,
callused fingers scrubbed dimes
with mercury to make them shine,
answering machines had no answers.

Everyone wanted something from someone
who was unreachable, the accountants
indicated zero, the plebiscite had not
been held yet government officials
surrounded us in the patio. All this

was just the morning. The sun flared
in cups of latte, the ambivalent,
questioning geese got lost in parking lots
and the guards shot at them. No one was hit.
No one was late. We were accomplices.

Caller

Who, having answered
a doorbell and found no one,
does not wonder about destiny?

If this time, maybe,
a saint has come
dressed like yourself
to take you
where you're supposed to go?

You miss him, later,
at work, lost
with the others
who move
in dim cubicles.

You miss him now,
sitting in the bar alone.
Music is not the miracle it was.
Maybe you can forget
the feeling that ran

a finger up your neck
as you stood there
in the windy doorway,
the thief's memory
of having escaped.

Homeless

He was an ascetic by virtue of
all his rejections and also by virtue
of his devotion to the real.
 -Wallace Stevens on Gustave Courbet

You came for pleasure, but the bum
slouched in a corner of the parking lot
winked and said, "You'll be sorry,"
when you handed him the keys
to your Volvo, you were late
and the hairy usher seated you
at the margins, but you tipped him
anyway, and shook his hand. Now
someone draped in shadows
has slunk into the neighbor seat.
You can smell him, hear him wheezing.
At the end of the show, you may
have to open your wallet,
give the stranger everything
you've got. Maybe what you've brought
is enough. Maybe you can fake it
with a card or two, a handful
of coins. Maybe he buys it,
and you get off easy. Or maybe,
seeing how little you've offered,
he wants everything. Can you imagine
returning with nothing left? You will have to
go to work for him, washing the pots
he's soiled, tending his indifferent
children. Can you take it, this
reduction of the world to an after-state,
these cold parameters, this oblivion
of now? Where did they go, the ghosts
who used to inhabit it with you?

They were sitting there, in the next row,
easy as picnickers, even laughing,
then they vanished. Can you still feel
their breath on your neck? Can you start over?

Poison

The element of silence
combined with time

The admixture of envy
and emptiness

The tincture of hatred
laced with grief

III. LAWS OF SILENCE

Pond, Winter

There are no big-shot Buddhas in nature
　　　　　　　　—Ikkyu

i.

The small division of snow
has cleansed the air
for three days and nights

ii.

Loss and gain are calculated
in the whisper
of pines at the window

iii.

Little tongues of threat

iv.

In this neighborhood
the price of property
is ice

v.

An accordion of secrets
opens, closes, opens
in your ear

vi.

Moon bright as paste
Owls jettison what doesn't please them

vii.

Your lungs, now

As They Say

When the heart breaks,
there's a socket

asymmetric as a fist.
Silences take longer.

Words stop in your throat.
Metaphors thin and fade.

They can digest nothing.
Poems, therefore, fail you,

sentenced, as you are, to truth.
Love is what they always

said it was:
a cause lost before joining.

The race of brothers and sisters
does not include you.

Atlantic

In legends, poets live by water.
Finn, when he was young,
learned poetry from Finegas
at the Boinn, where the poet
sat seven years to see
the salmon of knowledge
and, when it appeared at last,
Finn cooked it for him
over a peat fire, blistering
his thumb to get the pink meat right,
delicate as a just-lit coal.

Water is what earth needs,
to get it started.

Geysers of words
gush through the minds of the mad,
pumpkins piling their fields like waterwheels,
orange heads without faces.

As a boy, I swam out underwater—
easily as an otter from a pier,
I vanished despite warnings,
watching my parents disappear

above the wavering line
that divides one world from another,
tracing my body's shadows in the undertow,
my ears alive to my own breathing,
my lungs packed tight
with everything I needed

The Mormon trail
begins in pumpkins
and ends in water

        ·

At Steel Pier, the girl in sequins on the white horse
dived and vanished into spray.

From the boardwalk,
I watched them folded into waves

and watched them rise, a single body
with skin of salt.

        ·

Water is prophecy, the syllable you will gain
when your tongue proves itself,
the sleeve you will enter into.

Pleiades

The daughters of Atlas
turned to stone
then to stars,

who knows how?
They fall to earth
sometimes, missing

a familiar touch.
I miss my daughter,
who took her heart

so far away,
where love is thinned
to polar ice

that crusts and breaks and damages.
Some say the sky
is the abode of spirits

freed from time.
On Earth our only atmosphere
envelops us

the way tall buildings
shield the sun from streets
where travelers are thrust against a stream.

Seen from above,
everything that is
is heartless.

Years Ago

When I thought I wanted
to own my words
instead of being owned by the words of others,

when I thought that was possible,
I lost myself in books as in a foreign country.
I made a system—

Blakean, I know, but what's original?
Words counted most,
language more than people,

syllables more than feelings.
I walked around like a figure on the moon.
I was happy, the way, I thought, Flaubert

must have been happy,
hunting words in fields of his own mind
or Nabokov chasing colors that dance.

What's wrong with this is that it always fails,
like leaping off an alp to catch a salmon,
or falling on the tracks to stop a train.

The sorrow of this is simple:
Those who wrestle death in everything,
imagine love will outwit oblivion,

imagine it matters what they once wanted,
for no reason.
There's death in that too.

Delta

You must keep a careful eye on distance
because it grows,

you must watch the light draining
into the ocean carefully

because it's slippery as the ocean
which can swallow

the whole Mississippi
the way that subtle instrument,

your heart, swallows
everyone you have loved.

Caress

The Zen poet Ikkyu, four-
teenth century master,
loved sex, eating octopus,
drinking rice wine. This was his way
of celebrating being.
This is another thing Buddha
was wrong about, he thought
as he embraced his lover's body.

He knew poetry might lead to hell,
but he loved its beauties
the way he loved his penis,
holding it alone at night in an empty bed
and remembering Lady Mori's embrace
which was as good as any poem.
Death, of course, is unswervable,
but loneliness is worse.

Laws of Silence

i.

The way glass in a stream
hurls light at you
filtering nothing, reproducing
the daggers that dwell
inside everything

while the world pours
under it, stony,
accumulative, organized
only by what it quickly
overwhelms,

so you stare stock-still
and stare again until the fever
of looking is past and
you drift off in fragments,
cauterized, disassembled—

ii.

The way she is now, broken
& dangerous, the way her hair
flies out, twisted and leaking

is the second punctuation,
the only syntax

a carousel of stones
you find yourself on

iii.

"An unerring sense"—what do they mean?
A teaspoon dipped in the cup
of thought, a slow soliloquy
speeded to warp so that
decision reminds itself later
how it made its own endings?
What sense does not err? The cat's
chipped eye unravels on a toy,
the Roman temple collapses
despite its many architects
as the earth shifts elsewhere,
and she—her brimming dress,
her careless hat, her last
firm gesture of goodbye—
a leaf tossed backward
by the wind

iv.

Rainwater running
off the edges of leaves,
off the tips heavy
with thick commas
that will spill
into the spongy earth
and be absorbed

Ink making sounds
on paper
the way a memory
scratches itself
into silence,

long thumb of pain
stretching through time

v.

I remember you
waiting to meet me
in the empty corridor

where I never came

Application Guidelines

We understand
that all the preparation
you endured
was aimed at more,
that your accomplishments
can't be summed up by name.
Nevertheless, you must control
the urge to embellish
what must have been simple,
after all, a matter
of wants and calculations,
an easy thermometer
of pleasures and pain
and persistence in
what yielded nothing.
So keep it brief.
Remember, it's not
the stories you tell
that define you, it's
what you want.

SAVOR

Soul and body, Orpheus and Pan
converse with harp and flute
in Mozart's great concerto,
a wealth of notes cascading into air
like C-Major fireflies
exploding and dying.

When a poet says *body*,
it means too many things
to catalog, despite
staid mentors who teach you
not to say it at all:
Too familiar, too abstract, a site

indefinable as a clove.
Yet like a clove it nourishes,
it can be touched, stroked,
ground, nuzzled, poisoned,
smelled, inhaled, ruined.
It adds spice to things.

Craved for, it is music,
nevertheless, a burden.
Deeply cut by blades,
it weeps and drains.
Tasted, it flourishes
before it vanishes.

Things You Learn at Night

The laws of loss,
irremediable as heartache
but permanent.

The laws of breathing
in which one breath
must follow another breath.

The laws of memory
in which nothing
is finished.

The laws of terror
which involve
all of the above.

Hamlet Weds Ophelia

Think of them in bed together,
hooked into one shape,
parts of a sentence,
a single utterance
you can't unsay
even if you said everything,

against what would tabloids rage?
Against Love, that pulls together
what origin sets apart,
saying, *this, this,* and *this*—
meaning only, meaning *never*,
against Fate,

whose wisdom is to parse
what Love connects, breaking it and
breaking it again, and breaking
into the very center,
where what we want
becomes what we shouldn't—

all the ghosts behind all the curtains
revealed at last, stepping slowly out,
a chorus of skeletons acknowledged
as our sisters, our brothers in this night
(hear the courtier's sardonic laugh),
a *danse macabre* with tambourines.

This Room

The unutterable grows from music
the way music grows in an expanding wave,
Elgar's elegies or a concerto
for piano and oboe and orchestra
or a cello in the fingers of a master,
everyone knows that's sad,

especially the silences between notes
when after-music fills you and you wait
for the next note to take you,
a racing piano, strings,
something opening in the heart
where you can find again

the lost faces, the echoes
that are always with you, that at any moment
can become more stunning than sounds
gathered and flung like filigree,
and I remember why I wanted
to be here, in this quiet room.

Acknowledgments

Barrow Street: "Driving Home During the Eclipse," "Photo of a Field at the Start of a Century," "Gun," "Wrench," "Knife"

Beloit Poetry Journal: "Rope"

Hubbub: "Pond, Winter" (as "Pond, November")

The Iowa Review: "Caller," "Object /Lessons"

The Laurel Review: "Homeless"

Poetry Midwest: "Application Guidelines," "The Stain"

White Pelican Review: "Atlantic"

"Laws of Flight: I" also appeared as a single poem entitled "Flight" in *Five Colors,* published by CustomWords (Cincinnati:2004).

Stan Sanvel Rubin lives in Port Townsend on the Olympic Peninsula of Washington. He has published two previous full-length collections, *Midnight* (State Street Press) and *Five Colors* (CustomWords), and his poetry has appeared in such magazines as *The Georgia Review, Kenyon Review, Virginia Quarterly Review, Mississippi Review, Chelsea, Beloit Poetry Journal, Poetry Northwest, The Laurel Review* and many others. For over twenty years, he served as director of the Brockport Writers Forum and Videotape Library at SUNY Brockport, where he was co-editor of *The Post-Confessionals: Conversations with American Poets of the Eighties* (Associated University Presses). He received a 2002 Grant in Poetry from the Constance Saltonstall Foundation for the Arts, and his essay-reviews appear regularly in *Water~Stone Review.* He is founding director of the Rainier Writing Workshop low-residency MFA Program at Pacific Lutheran University.